PEOPLE WHO **HELP** US

At the
Hospital

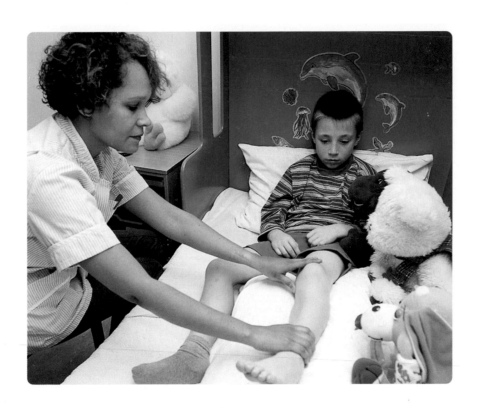

Deborah Chancellor

Photographs: Chris Fairclough

W

FRANKLIN WATTS
LONDON · SYDNEY

 This symbol is often seen on ambulances and medical signs. The snake and staff (the stick in the middle) are the symbols of Asclepius, the Ancient Greek god of healing.

First published in 2003 by
Franklin Watts
96 Leonard Street
London
EC2A 4XD

Franklin Watts Australia
45–51 Huntley Street
Alexandria
NSW 2015

A CIP catalogue record for this book is available from the British Library.

ISBN 0 7496 4901 1

Series Editor: Jackie Hamley
Cover Design: Peter Scoulding
Design: Ian Thompson

Photos
All commissioned photographs by Chris Fairclough.
The publishers would like to thank the following
for permission to use photographs:
John Birdsall Photo Library 21 (top), 24 (top)

Every attempt has been made to clear copyright. Should there be any inadvertent omission, please apply to the publisher for rectification.

The author and publisher would especially like to thank the staff at The Royal Berkshire Hospital for giving their help and time so generously.

Printed in Malaysia

Contents

Meet the team

We go to hospital when we are very ill, when we need special medical help, or if we have been badly hurt in an accident.

Doctors, nurses and many other people work together in hospitals to help us get well again. The Royal Berkshire is a hospital in Reading. Over four thousand people work there.

This is the main entrance to the Royal Berkshire Hospital.

There are about eight hundred beds for patients at the Royal Berkshire Hospital. The beds are in large rooms called **wards**.

These people all work in a children's ward called Dolphin Ward. Some of them look after the patients. Others help in different ways.

Some of the staff on Dolphin Ward.

1. Carl (**porter**) **2.** Dean (theatre porter)
3. Mary (cleaner) **4.** Michelle (**ward clerk**)
5. Louise (**staff nurse**) **6.** Alison (**ward sister**)
7. Steve (staff nurse) **8.** Jill (doctor)
9. Becky (**student nurse**) **10.** Laura (ward clerk).

The hospital

☺ **Hospitals are big places, and it can be hard to find your way around. When visitors arrive, they go to the main reception desk.**

The security guard checks the identity card of a visiting doctor.

Linda is a **receptionist**. She tells people which part of the hospital they need to go to, and gives directions.

A security guard works with Linda. He makes sure the hospital staff, patients and buildings are kept safe.

Visitors use this plan to help them find the ward or department they are looking for.

There are many departments at the hospital. The departments specialise in different things, for example maternity is for mothers and new babies, **intensive care** is for very sick patients, and **geriatrics** is for elderly patients.

Many people come to the hospital to visit a friend or relative in one of the wards. There is a flower shop near the reception desk where they can buy flowers for the patient.

The florist makes beautiful bouquets for patients.

Visitors are not allowed to eat or drink in the hospital wards. If they are hungry or thirsty, they can go to the visitor café.

The café is next to the flower shop.

FACT

▷ Number of departments in the hospital: 38

▷ Department that sees most patients per day: Accident and Emergency

▷ Number of wards in the hospital: 21

▷ Number of children's wards in the hospital: 4

Accident and Emergency

One of the busiest departments at the hospital is "Accident and Emergency". People come here if they have been injured, had an accident, or have become ill very suddenly.

Some people are rushed to hospital by **ambulance**. There is a special place for the ambulances to park, just outside Accident and Emergency.

This ambulance has brought a patient to the hospital.

Matthew hurt his leg when he fell off his skateboard. He has just arrived at Accident and Emergency. Matthew is using a wheelchair, because it is too painful for him to walk.

The receptionist at Accident and Emergency asks Matthew's name and the details of his accident.

A nurse looks at Matthew's leg to see how bad his injury is. Matthew will need more medical help. The nurse asks Matthew to wait until a doctor is ready to see him.

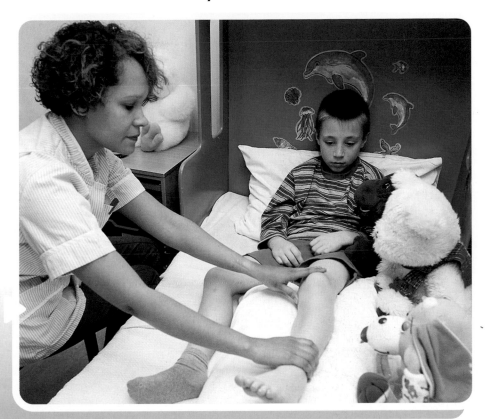

Christina asks Matthew some more questions about his accident.

A student nurse called Christina shows Matthew to the children's area of Accident and Emergency. He lies on a bed while he waits for the doctor.

The doctor thinks Matthew has broken his ankle. Matthew is sent to have an **x-ray** of his leg.

> *On a normal day in Accident and Emergency, about 180 people come in to see us for treatment.*
>
> **Brenda, lead sister in Accident and Emergency**

X-rays and plaster casts

X-rays show what has happened under the skin. If a patient has broken a bone, he or she may need a plaster cast and more help.

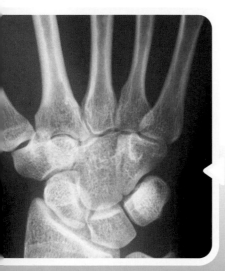

People who give patients x-rays are called **radiographers**. A radiographer called Shelley asks Matthew to lie on a special table under her x-ray machine.

X-rays show inside the body and help doctors to see what is wrong with bones.

A special covering protects parts of Matthew's body that do not need to be x-rayed.

Shelley works the x-ray machine from behind a screen.

Shelley takes lots of x-rays. Each x-ray produces a tiny amount of **radiation**. It would not be safe for Shelley to have so many small doses of radiation, so she stands behind a screen to take x-rays.

Matthew's x-ray shows that he has broken his ankle.
The doctor in Accident and Emergency sends Matthew
to the plaster room to have a **plaster cast** put on his leg.

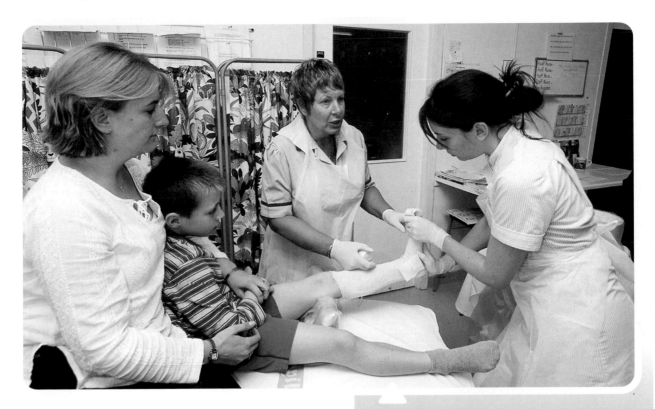

Matthew keeps his leg still so the nurses can work more easily.

Maddie is the senior staff nurse in the plaster room. She wraps Matthew's ankle in a wet plaster bandage, which dries and becomes stiff. The plaster cast holds Matthew's ankle in the right position and helps it to heal properly.

"Children's broken bones mend quite quickly. A child with a broken leg usually needs to wear a plaster cast for about 8 weeks."

Maddie, senior staff nurse in the plaster room

The children's ward

☺ **Children who need to stay in hospital usually go to a children's ward. This kind of ward is called a "paediatric ward".**

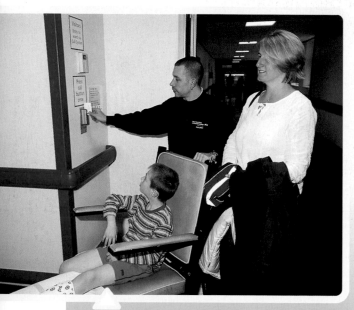

Carl uses his identity card to swipe through the security lock. This opens the door to the ward.

Matthew has broken his ankle quite badly. He needs to have an **operation** to make sure the **fracture** heals properly. He is admitted to a children's ward in the hospital.

Carl, a porter, takes Matthew to Dolphin Ward. Carl's job is to push patients in wheelchairs or on trolleys along the hospital corridors, to take them where they need to go.

Michelle is the ward clerk on duty at the reception desk. She welcomes patients to Dolphin Ward.

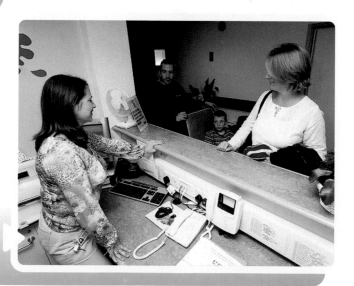

Michelle welcomes Matthew and his mum to the ward.

Children in hospital do not need to miss out on any school. Friendly teachers visit the ward every day to work with them.

Carol, the teacher, reads a book with Matthew while the nurses ask his mum for some details.

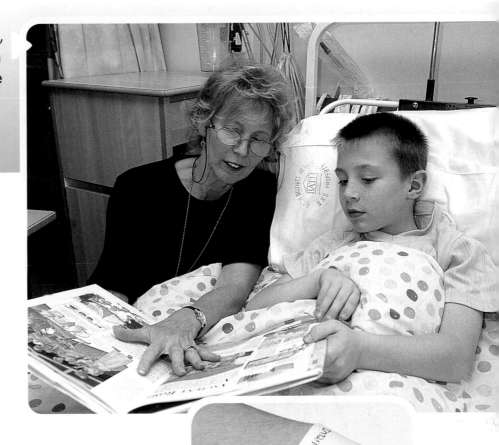

Matthew does not have to stay on his own in hospital. A staff nurse called Steve tells Matthew's mum that she can stay overnight if she wants to.

Steve shows Matthew's mum to the parents' and carers' bedroom, next to the ward.

Matthew's name, date of birth and the name of the ward are written on a tag, which is fixed around his wrist. He will wear this throughout his stay in hospital.

Nurses

😊 **Nurses in hospitals are trained to look after the patients. They care for their patients, following the doctors' instructions.**

The nurses in Dolphin Ward often have meetings to discuss the needs of their patients. The meetings take place at a desk called "the nurses' station".

Staff nurses Louise and Steve do some paperwork at the nurses' station.

When Matthew arrives in Dolphin Ward, the nurses do all they can to make him feel happy and relaxed. Staff nurse Steve chats to Matthew while he checks his temperature.

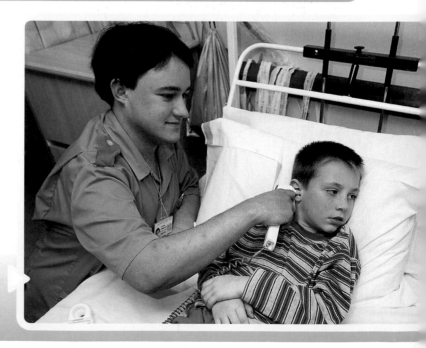

This thermometer measures Matthew's temperature through his ear.

Staff nurses look after the patients in the ward. One of their most important jobs is to give out medicines to the patients. They do this at regular times every day.

Staff nurse Steve gives Matthew some medicine to stop his leg hurting.

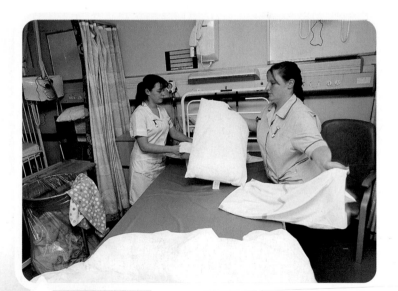

The bedding is changed every day, so germs cannot spread around the ward.

Nurses train for more than three years to become fully qualified. Student nurses like Becky work in the wards to get experience. They also help out with useful jobs, such as changing the bedding.

" *When I do a night shift, I start work at half past eight in the evening. I leave to go home at a quarter past seven in the morning!*
Steve, staff nurse in Dolphin Ward "

Doctors

☺ **Lots of different doctors work at the hospital. Some doctors are experts in children's health.**

Each child in Dolphin Ward has a doctor who looks after them while they are in hospital. The doctors usually visit their patients once a day. These visits are called **"ward rounds"**.

Matthew's doctor has just arrived at Dolphin Ward to do her ward round.

FACT

▷ *Number of doctors at the hospital: 141*

▷ *Number of surgeons at the hospital: 31*

▷ *Average number of operations per day at the hospital: 126*

Matthew is looked after by a **paediatric doctor** called Jill. Jill is an expert at working with children, and she also specialises in **orthopaedics**, which means she knows a lot about bones and muscles. She talks with Matthew about his operation and tells him who the **surgeon** will be.

The doctors work closely with the nurses in Dolphin Ward. Staff nurses go on the ward rounds with the doctors, and update the notes about each patient. Brief patient notes are kept at the end of a patient's bed. The proper notes are kept safely at the nurses' station.

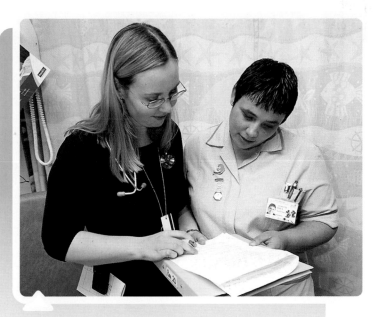

Matthew's doctor, Jill, discusses his treatment with staff nurse Annette.

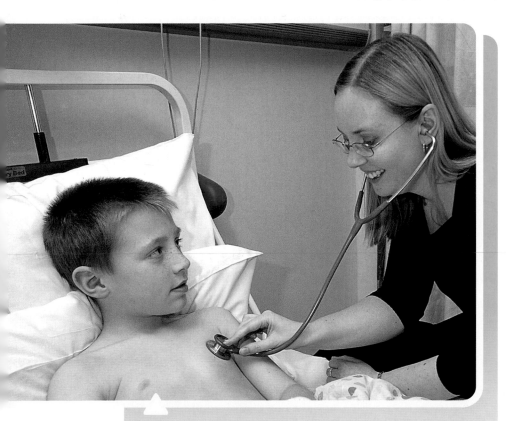

Jill uses a stethoscope to listen to Matthew's heart and lungs. Stethoscopes help doctors to hear sounds more easily.

Matthew's doctor checks his heartbeat. She wants to be sure Matthew is fit enough to have his operation the next day. If she is worried about anything, she will talk to Matthew's surgeon before Matthew has his operation.

Having an operation

Some patients need an operation to remove or repair a damaged part inside their body.

On the morning of Matthew's operation, he has a sign above his bed. The sign reminds the nurses not to give Matthew anything to eat or drink before his operation, as it would make him sick.

Please do not give me anything to eat or drink.

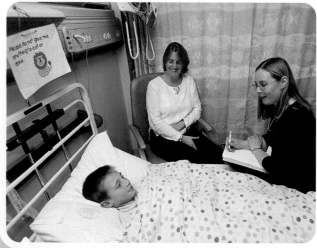

Matthew is not allowed to eat or drink anything for at least six hours before his operation.

When it is time for Matthew's operation, he is given some medicine to help him relax. Carl, the porter, wheels Matthew to a room where a doctor gives him an **anaesthetic**. This sends him into a deep sleep.

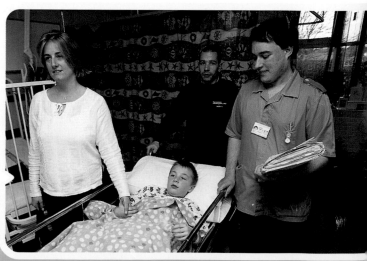

Matthew is pushed out of the ward on a trolley. He is wearing a theatre gown, ready for his operation.

Matthew is taken to an **operating theatre**, where a surgeon performs the operation on his leg. When the surgeon has finished, a new plaster cast is put on Matthew's ankle.

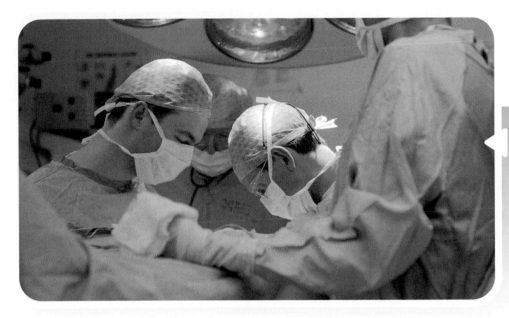

The surgical team wear gowns, gloves, masks and hats to keep everything in the operating theatre **sterile**.

After the operation, Matthew wakes up in his bed back in Dolphin Ward. He feels hungry, so he asks for some toast. He is allowed to eat now!

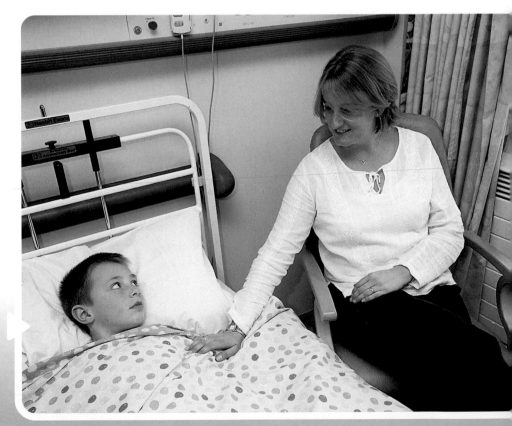

When Matthew wakes up after his anaesthetic, his mum is by his bedside.

Play time

☺ **Children in Dolphin Ward are encouraged to play a lot. Playing is not just fun; it can also help sick patients get better.**

Just after his operation, Matthew does not feel like getting out of bed. A **play leader** called Sarah brings some paints to his bedside.

Play leaders play with the children, to help them enjoy their stay in hospital.

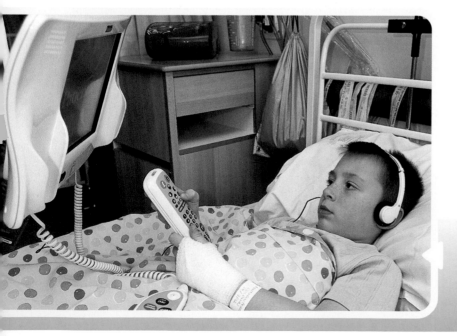

Dolphin Ward has been specially designed for young patients, to make their stay in hospital as much fun as possible.

Each bed has a TV screen, so children can watch their favourite programmes or use the Internet.

Physiotherapists help patients become active again after an illness or injury. Gill, the physiotherapist, shows Matthew how to use crutches so he can walk more easily with his plaster cast.

Matthew will have to exercise his good leg while his broken ankle mends.

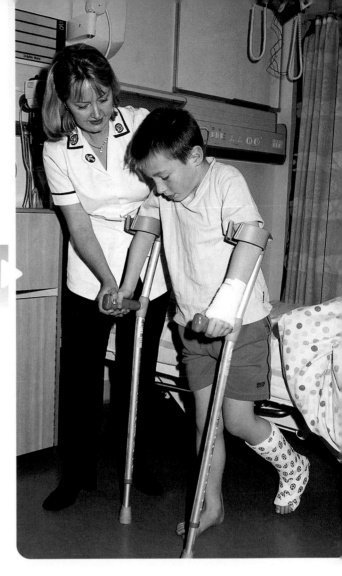

Sarah, the play leader, builds a house with Matthew.

As soon as Matthew gets used to his crutches, he goes to the playroom on the ward. The play leaders play with the children in the playroom.

Sometimes when children arrive on the ward they are a bit sad. When it is time to leave, they have enjoyed themselves so much they don't want to go home!
Sarah, play leader

Meal times

At meal times, food is brought to the wards from the main hospital kitchen.

Hospital patients can look at a menu to choose what they want to eat. The food they have chosen is brought to the ward.

In the hospital kitchen, cooks prepare meals for the patients.

A kitchen porter brings the children's meals to Dolphin Ward. They are taken on a special trolley to the ward kitchen.

Marian, one of the helpers in Dolphin Ward, serves meals in the ward kitchen.

Children in Dolphin Ward can eat in the playroom if they want to. Patients who cannot get up can eat meals in their beds.

Matthew has got his appetite back after his operation.

Meal times on the ward can be messy! The ward must be kept very clean, so cleaners sweep and mop the floors after each meal time.

FACT

▷ *Hospital meal times:*
Breakfast 7.30–8.30am

Lunch   12 noon–1pm

Dinner   5–6pm

▷ *Meal choice:*

3-course hot or cold meals, including vegetarian and other special diets

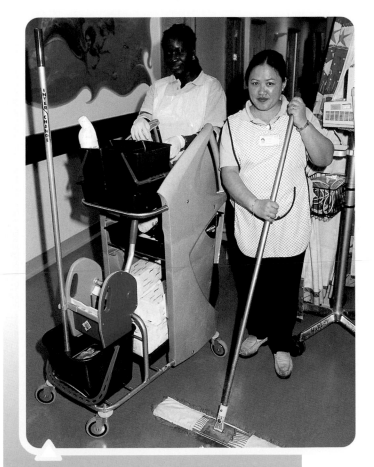

Mary and Janaki are cleaning up after lunch in Dolphin Ward.

A patient can only leave hospital when their doctor says they are well enough. The nurses then arrange for the patient to return home.

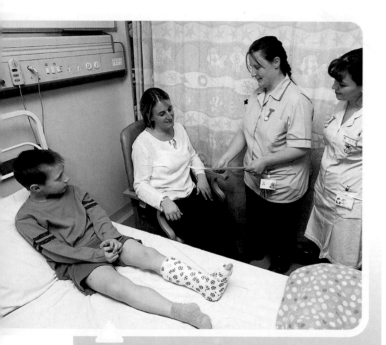

Matthew's doctor is happy with his progress. She tells the Dolphin Ward nurses that Matthew can be discharged. This means Matthew will be able to leave hospital later that day.

Staff nurse Louise gives Matthew's mum a leaflet about leaving hospital. Matthew will have to rest his leg when he gets home.

The time comes for Matthew to say goodbye to the nurses in Dolphin Ward.

Matthew has made some good friends in the ward.

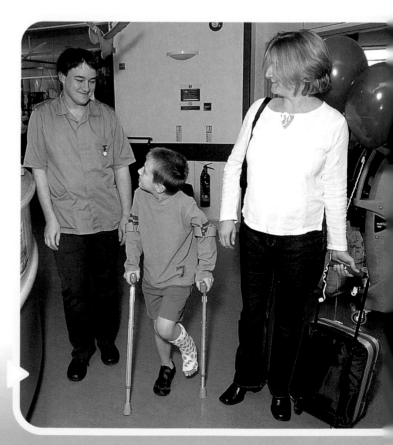

On the way out of the hospital, Matthew and his mum pass the **pharmacy**. Some patients need to take medicine with them when they leave hospital. They can pick this up from the hospital pharmacy.

Pharmacists and **dispensers** work at the pharmacy. They prepare medicines for the patients.

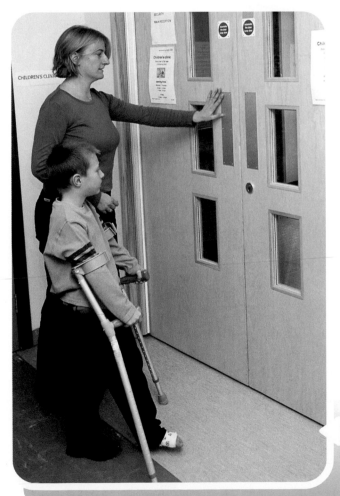

Matthew returns to hospital eight weeks later for an **outpatients** appointment at the children's clinic. He sees an orthopaedic doctor, who tells him that his ankle has healed very well. It is time to have his plaster cast taken off at last!

Matthew won't have to wear his plaster cast for much longer.

Emergency!

It is very important to stay calm in an emergency.

Only call for an ambulance in a real emergency. Ambulance crews are very busy, and a hoax call might cost someone else their life.

HOW TO CALL AN AMBULANCE

If you need to phone for an ambulance, do the following things:

1. Dial 999. You will be put through to the emergency services.
2. Ask for an ambulance.
3. Give the telephone number of the phone you are using.
4. Say where and when the emergency happened.
Give the address if you know it.
5. Describe the kind of emergency, for example a road accident.
6. Say how many people have been hurt, how old they are and whether they are male or female.
7. Describe the condition of the injured people.
8. Explain any possible dangers, such as gas leaks or fog.

The ambulance will arrive as soon as possible, thanks to you.

FIRST AID

First aid is the care given to a sick or injured person before a doctor or an ambulance crew arrive. It can make the difference between life and death for the injured person.

Anyone can give first aid – it could be a member of the family, a friend or even a stranger who happens to be there. Be prepared for an emergency by learning how to give first aid properly. To find out more, contact the St. John Ambulance organisation. (See page 30.)

Glossary

Ambulance A vehicle that brings sick or injured people to hospital.

Anaesthetic A drug given to patients before an operation so they don't feel any pain.

Dispenser A person who gives out medicines to patients in a pharmacy.

Fracture A cracked or broken bone.

Geriatrics The care of elderly patients.

Intensive care A hospital ward for very ill people who need lots of special medical help.

Operating theatre A room in a hospital where operations happen.

Operation A medical treatment in which a patient's body is cut open to remove or repair a damaged part.

Orthopaedics A special kind of medical study, looking at bones.

Outpatients Patients who visit a hospital to see a doctor, but who do not stay in the hospital.

Paediatric doctor A children's doctor.

Pharmacist A person trained to prepare medicines.

Pharmacy A place where medicines are stored and given to patients.

Physiotherapist Somebody who is trained to help patients become fit after an illness or operation.

Plaster cast A hard plaster dressing that holds a broken bone in the correct position while it heals.

Play leader Someone who helps children to play and relax.

Porter A person who moves patients and equipment around a hospital.

Radiation A type of energy given out by x-rays.

Radiographer Somebody who is trained to give patients x-rays.

Receptionist Somebody who helps patients or visitors as they arrive.

Staff nurse A qualified nurse who looks after patients on a ward.

Sterile Clean and free of germs.

Student nurse Someone who is training to become a nurse.

Surgeon A doctor who is trained to carry out operations on patients.

Ward A large room where patients stay in hospital.

Ward clerk Someone in charge of admitting new patients to a ward.

Ward round Regular visits made by doctors to their patients in a ward.

Ward sister A senior nurse in charge of a ward.

X-ray A photograph of the inside of a patient's body, made by x-rays (small rays that "see" through skin).

Further information

To find out more about children's hospitals, visit the Great Ormond Street Hospital website at: www.goshkids.nhs.uk

To find out more about children's health in Australia, visit the Children's Health Development Foundation at: www.chdf.org.au

Note to parents and teachers: Every effort has been made by the Publishers to ensure that these websites are suitable for children; that they are of the highest educational value, and that they contain no inappropriate or offensive material. However, because of the nature of the Internet, it is impossible to guarantee that the contents of these sites will not be altered. We strongly advise that Internet access is supervised by a responsible adult.

To learn about first aid, contact the St. John Ambulance Society:

St. John Ambulance
National Headquarters
27, St. John's Lane
London EC1M 4BU

Tel: 08700 10 49 50
Or visit:
www.sja.org.uk/young_people

St. John Ambulance Australia
PO Box 3895
Manuka ACT 2605
Or visit: www.stjohn.org.au

Index